Contradictions -
Bringing The Past Forward
Art + Humanities Installation by barbara Gothard

Title Panel: *Contradictions - Bringing The Past Forward*
San Bernardino County Museum
February 8 - April 21, 2022

Contradictions –
Bringing The Past Forward
Art + Humanities Installation by

barbara Gothard

an exhibition presented by

SAN BERNARDINO COUNTY MUSEUM

REDLANDS, CALIFORNIA

CONTENTS

This book is dedicated to Donny and Ann Marie Gothard, my never-ending sources of pride and inspiration, and to Diana Rodriguez, Grace, Georgina, Justin, Jonah, and Isaiah Gothard.

To my extended family and friends for whose support and encouragement I'm very appreciative and to those who deal with today's challenges in the aftermath of history.

And to Kosen Rufu, spreading world peace through individual happiness.

Contradictions –
Bringing The Past Forward

Visual interpretation honoring the legacy
of twenty-three African American homesteaders
who settled in the far Eastern Mojave Desert in 1910

In *Contradictions - Bringing The Past Forward©*, artist Barbara Gothard visually interprets and honors the legacy of twenty-three African American Homesteaders, who settled in the Eastern Mojave Desert in 1910, in the context of her own lived experience as an African American female artist living in the desert, sharing their stories via public presentations.

The research-based multimedia Arts + Humanities installation, first exhibited at San Bernardino County Museum in 2021, consists of twenty-three digital paintings created with the software ProCreate on her iPad, which she began exploring in 2017 as an extension of her oil painting practice. These paintings, printed on Senso raw linen canvas with a process she pioneered in the desert in 2020 in conjunction with Stephen Baumbach Photography and are combined with an installation of the replica of the 1910 tract map of the Lanfair Valley area, a story map created by ESRI staff Doug Morgenthaler and Jim Herries, images of related archival documents, and Lanfair/Dunbar archeological objects loaned by Mojave National Preserve. Gothard's visual illumination of the lives of these homesteaders is believed to be the first and the only time in more than 100 years that their stories are portrayed in a visual format. The artworks inform a series of artist talks and community discussion hosted by public and nonprofit organizations and on social media.

Gothard's journey began in late 2019 while searching for information about a different topic when she discovered a *Daily Bulletin* article by Joe Blackstock about these African American Homesteaders. The article included an ad from the May 10, 1910 *Los Angeles Herald*. In response to this newspaper ad specifically recruiting "colored" homesteaders, 23 families became western settlers in far eastern San Bernardino County. Blackstock's article became the impetus for Gothard's project, *Contradictions - Bringing The Past Forward©,* along with the generous support, encouragement, and dialog with the Mojave Preserve staff and the "pioneer researcher" credited as the initial information source.

Gothard's challenge over a three year period was to develop artworks that convey the homesteaders's stories while not only being true to her own oeuvre, but also the contradiction of using a digital painting format to visually convey stories from 1910. Gothard's invitation from BoxoPROJECTS Artist Residency provided the perfect desert studio environment in Joshua Tree, California for her to develop the prototype for the installation, without distractions, through a framework of change, continuity, diversity, cause and effect, interconnectedness, community, identity, and belonging in the context of social, political, economic, cultural, and environmental factors prevalent in the early 20th century in the United States. The artworks in *Contradictions - Bringing The Past Forward* explore themes of hope, disillusionment, and strong family bonds based on archival research and interviews.

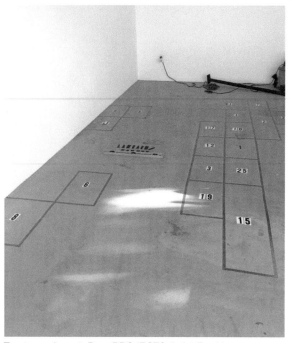

Studio, BoxoPROJECTS Artist Residency, 2022

Tract map layout, BoxoPROJECTS Artist Residency, Joshua Tree, CA 2021

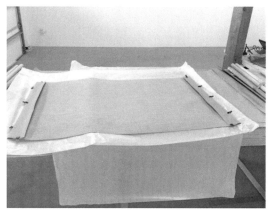

Artwork Construction, BoxoPROJECTS Artist Residency, Joshua Tree, CA 2021

Artist at work, BoxoPROJECTS Artist Residency Joshua Tree, CA 2021

Photo Credit: Bernard Liebov

Artwork Construction, BoxoPROJECTS Artist Residency, Joshua Tree, CA 2021

A Beacon of Light

Anytime we can shine a light exposing the myth of our absence in American history, we as African Americans can take prideful steps toward better understanding and appreciating our history, and further educating others as we relay the contributions of the many who came before us.

Barbara Gothard's solo exhibition *Contradictions - Bringing the Past Forward (Contradictions)* is a beacon of light commanding our attention. She began her exploration by delving into a 1910 newspaper advertisement recruiting homesteaders to move to Lanfair Valley, where they would mine and homestead in the far Eastern Mojave Desert of Southern California. The ad was directed solely at African Americans.

Barbara's research and stunning artwork traces some of the people who answered the ad, and come they did from throughout the United States. As I heard so often from African Americans who left their homes in the south, they simply reckoned the life they envisioned couldn't be as bad as the life they were living. During the early 1900s, the notion of leaving for a better life began to take root, first by word-of-mouth, and then through newspapers in other parts of America as workers were needed in the north and west with the expansion of manufacturing and later the burgeoning automobile industry.

Barbara applied her research and investigative skills to the project in 2019-2020. In 2021, continuing her search for information on the minority homesteaders, Barbara uncovered a trove of government records with maps and property lines. Original artifacts uncovered by Mojave National Preserve archeologists bearing witness to a simple life were loaned to San Bernardino County Museum for Barbara's exhibit. And, for a few homesteaders, it was also the religious life of the Seventh Day Adventists.

In her quest to fully understand the life and times over 100 years ago, Barbara seeks, finds and interviews pioneer researchers and others who had conducted oral histories about their community in Lanfair Valley. Knowing the depth of the commitment of my dear friend and fellow artist to this project, those interviews had a profound impact on her and, as we see, onto the artworks she creates for this exhibition.

The substantial data that Barbara uncovered gave her the fortitude to boldly step outside her artistic comfort zone—where much admired work has been produced— and create artworks uniquely whispering the plight of these individual settlers from their distant past.

Now comes my question…

Who among us working artists would take such a fearless stance on a *new* course of artistic expression with a major exhibition at a museum on the line? I suspect not many of us.

The typical museum gallery design gives rise to Barbara's idea of representing the homesteaders by creating individual wall hangings. She infuses subdued color palettes reflecting the desert's omnipresent lights and the flower representing the home state of each person. A map with the person's Lanfair Valley property line is included in the wall hanging, accompanied by a small card with detailed information. The past and present make themselves oddly comfortable in the same artwork space.

Artist Talk and Exhibit, BoxoPROJECTS Artist Residency Joshua Tree, CA 2021 Photo Credit: Bernard Liebov

This juxtaposition makes me want to know more. With no photographs offering visual representation, it's an opportunity for the viewer to use their own 'artistic eye' to visualize day-to-day life with the information Barbara has represented.

Affixing a map in brightly color-coded tape onto the museum gallery floor, Barbara reveals more information as we begin to see the *Contradictions* of an idyllic life. Mirroring familiar situations that were showing up in other states, the division of property lines are telling us in glaring government records that the property lines of Lanfair Valley were, indeed, based on the color of one's skin and on the wishes of one of the patriarchs who wanted his family members to be located near him.

Thinking these kinds of things happened is a different reaction from seeing the actual evidence which sets off an emotional jolt to my gut—just knowing some of the treatment endured by our ancestors.

The emotional pull of this exhibition may make some viewers feel as though they had stepped upon hallowed ground as one might feel walking in a cemetery near the grave of a loved one. Or, the wall hangings may conjure up the very existence of those who once lived the life described herein. With our ever-evolving attitudes on race in America, I can only hope a peacefulness has now descended on the homesteaders' land, a peace that was perhaps never felt while they lived.

The exhibition richly adds to our understanding in subtle and overt ways as to how the Lanfair community came to be, what transpired when new arrivals settled into daily routines, and then much is left to our imagination. During the emotional days of endurance in their farmland, they must have faced the same issues confronting the cities they had come from, as those issues had now morphed throughout the United States.

Working the mines and tilling the soil under unforgiving climatic conditions coupled with an unfriendly social environment brought these issues to the fore. Many in the region disclose the same is true today. The lack of rainfall is playing havoc in most areas of California. The social environment has progressed with the enactment of laws which don't allow discrimination in the work place, public spaces, transportation or housing, and yet, the present-day news reports seem filled to overflowing with crimes perpetrated by one person or group against another solely based on one's race.

Artist Talk and Exhibit, BoxoPROJECTS Artist Residency Joshua Tree, CA 2021 Photo Credit: Bernard Liebov

During the first years of the 1900s, not far removed from the generations of enslaved black people, the Civil War, and the signing of the Emancipation Proclamation, the general sentiment in America was to keep the races separate in all ways and always.

Early American history books seldom acknowledged the accomplishments of our ancestors, but now with the in-depth research and factual evidence unearthed, more recent books leave little speculation about the role African Americans had in building our country from its infancy. We as a people were not only working the cotton fields and orange groves in the south, but managed to become well-known and respected builders, craftsmen, statesmen, authors, educators, musicians, artists, bankers, shop keepers, lawyers, inventors, preachers and soldiers in the fields of war...to name a few.

My memories and many of my own works of art embody the stories repeated and echoed by our elders, who were part of what is now considered "the great migration." From the early 1900's to the 1970's, over seven million black people made their way out of the south to parts in the north and west. This exodus included my grandparents who, with my father at four months old, moved from Montgomery, Alabama to Cleveland, Ohio. (They considered that their best decision. I consider moving to Los Angeles my smartest decision to date.)

I relate this story of the constant movement of black families because the news was assuredly affecting people from all economic and social stratagems of life, from the Atlantic to the Pacific, and Lanfair Valley could not have been immune to this insistent drum beat.

I have enormous appreciation for all the elements Barbara brought together so we might feel the presence of those who were here, making a difference. With newspaper archives, found objects from the Lanfair site, historical and educational references, personal interviews, plus guided by her creative and innate sense, she has shone a beacon of light which will forever burn.

The *Installation*

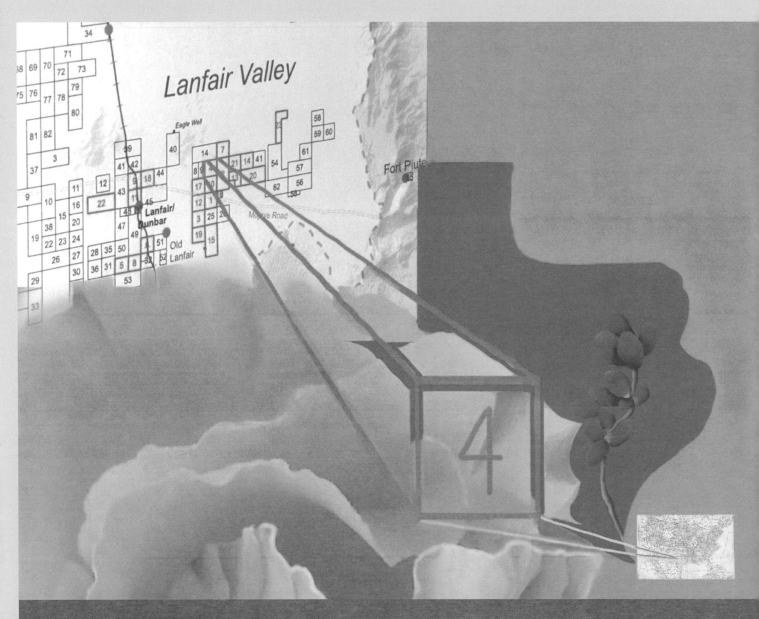

SAN BERNARDINO
COUNTY MUSEUM

2024 Orange Tree Lane • 909.798.8608 • Tuesday-Sunday, 9am-5pm
www.sbcounty.gov/museum • @SBCMuseum

Exhibition: *Contradictions - Bringing The Past Forward*
San Bernardino County Museum
February 8 - April 21, 2022

MELISSA RUSSO, Museum Director, San Bernardino County Museum

Transformational Exhibit Practice
Manifests in Barbara Gothard's *Contradictions*

In 2016, the San Bernardino County Museum revised its mission statement, from a very collection-centric statement to one more intentionally focused on public engagement, inquiry, and impact. That mission fully manifests in Barbara Gothard's installation *"Contradictions: Bringing the Past Forward"*. An innovative fusion of art, research, and historic preservation, Gothard's exploration of 23 California homesteaders is transformative and unique. Stories of African American homesteaders in California are virtually non-existent in museum galleries. To appreciate the value that "Contradictions" brings to the Museum, it is necessary to understand the historic context of the San Bernardino County Museum itself.

The Museum has led critical research and exhibited extensively on topics that promote the humanities, natural, and earth sciences since the 1950s. The Museum's vast history collection is a rich array of material culture, including indigenous anthropological artifacts, centered primarily in the 18th—20th century. The Museum's geology and paleontology collections comprise centuries of records from the region's notable public lands including Joshua Tree National Park and Mojave National Preserve where Gothard's subjects homesteaded in 1910.

Up until around the 1980s, the professionals who develop the stories in museums and provide society with "community anchors" convening spaces for educational enrichment in the arts and sciences – curators, exhibit developers, and writers – were trained in, and overwhelmingly drew from academic research. The peer-review practice can be problematic. Stereotypes or cultural assumptions can infect future iterations that draw on those original assumptions and perpetuate a worldview that is often incomplete or inaccurate.

Skewed narratives on gender and ethnicity, disproportionally centered on white males, made its way into curatorial practice and museum exhibitions. This practice contributed deeply to the notion that "whiteness" is the cultural norm; black American history and experience was rendered inconsequential, secondary, or invisible in museums.

Since its founding nearly 70 years ago, the San Bernardino County Museum amassed a collection of over three million artifacts, yet very little could be associated with the stories of African Americans, a population that currently makes up nearly 10% of the county. This bias in storytelling shaped an incomplete and inaccurate record of the development of our region, as the museum's programming was complicit in influencing opinions and standardizing prejudiced assumptions that favored a dominant culture.

Mojave National Preserve, 2021

Mojave Road Guide, Dennis G. Casebier, June 1986

Since its founding nearly 70 years ago, the San Bernardino County Museum amassed a collection of over three million artifacts, yet very little could be associated with the stories of African Americans, a population that currently makes up nearly 10% of the county. This bias in storytelling shaped an incomplete and inaccurate record of the development of our region, as the museum's programming was complicit in influencing opinions and standardizing prejudiced assumptions that favored a dominant culture.

The museum field's collective attention to bias in storytelling was aroused in 1992. That year, artist Fred Wilson proposed to the Maryland Historical Society what would give rise to the groundbreaking installation, "Mining the Museum." Wilson chose this partnership specifically because in earlier visits to the museum, he felt viscerally uncomfortable and unseen there.

A year-long research project deep in the museum's collection resulted in a radical exhibit that posed objects of slavery (manacles, whipping post) alongside, and in juxtaposition to, the cultural artifacts of white high society (silver vessels, dollhouse) starkly unearthing the symbols, relationships, and systems that supported the brutality of servitude.

Over the next thirty years, the museum field increasingly championed more diverse and inclusive storytelling, closely paralleling the rise in "public history" practice, which approaches interpretation of the past in a more populist and innovative fashion than traditional academic methods and places value on the vernacular aspects of society to document historical stories. Even before Black Lives Matter protests accelerated diversity initiatives in the museum field, the San Bernardino County Museum, like many others, had been building programs that sought to establish a more full and factual

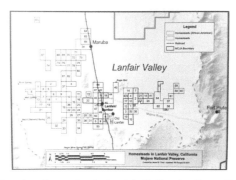
African American homesteads, Lanfair, California (Jesse Tune 2021)

account of the diverse history in our country and to expand representation to all of our region's inhabitants.

Thankfully, we are able draw on the inspiration of other groundbreakers, like Wilson's "Mining the Museum" work, as well as the expertise of a rising generation of public historians, preservationists, curators, and artists who embrace an expansive and sometimes messy view of history to reveal a more generous and complex narrative of society.

Austin Allen, in "Site of the Unseen: The Racial Gaming of the American Landscape," writes "The American landscape [in which African Americans are barely seen] hides how African Americans have built so much of the foundation of the United States; instead, it reveals historical inaccuracies.

Defining these places gives us a more accurate read of our country and offers a means to build a more relevant and equitable society. But first, it is important to understand the way African Americans have moved through the land, either by choice, or by outside force."

Gothard's "Contradictions" belongs in the continuum of artist historians unfolding and expanding our definition of the American experience. It is hard to overemphasize the significance of her stories about the Lanfair homesteaders, settling on the eastern edge of Mojave National Preserve.

A brutally hot environment during many months of the year, the landscape is covered in creosote bush, a nasty chaparral shrub that has thrived for thousands of years through cloning. The only evidence left of the once bustling town of Lanfair are the foundations of buildings that included homes and a post office. It is hard to imagine the heartiness required of these homesteaders who would face this unrelenting heat and an inhospitable landscape expected to offer farming and mining opportunities to the inhabitants.

Installation view with case and video

To tell this story, Gothard drew on the work of other researchers that came before her. Gothard's gift to our visitors is the creativity she employs to tell this powerful story. Through her inspired combination of symbols, maps, artifacts, and primary source illustrations, each individual homesteader emerges as having existed in our shared American past.

Objects- Lanfair, CA 1910 Objects

Walter Hood describes the "two-ness" of people that "live within the double." Specifically, Hood means African Americans who have engaged in society through the eyes of others, "the white narrative," but whose own lived experience – patterns and practices – reflects generations of Black culture that have been excluded from our "common" history. According to Hood, "all Americans can learn from people who have had to look at themselves with a two-ness. People should see that they themselves, and landscapes, have multiplicities. [Elements] in the landscape are needed so that all people can see reflections of themselves, like memories and mythologies embedded in places that highlight the two-ness. These places have been documented for centuries, as evidenced in maps, journals, and documentations bearing their names and place, yet they did not matter to our country's collective memory."

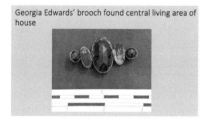

Georgia Edwards' brooch found central living area of house

Cottolene can lid, 35 meters NW Bronson house

In "Contradictions," Gothard's superpower is her "two-ness," skillfully connecting a modern public to the lives of these 23 African Americans. The installation invites visitors to see the Mojave Desert's past through a prism, redefining what homesteaders looked like, and including them in the documented history of successive waves of migrants looking for a better life for themselves and their families.

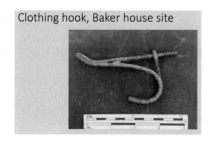

Clothing hook, Baker house site

For further reading, Kerr Houston's article "How Mining the Museumhanged the Art World," *Bmore Art*, May 3, 2017; Laura Raicovich, "What Happened When Fred Wilson Dug Beneath a Museum's Floorboards," *Hyperallergic*, Aug 16, 2019.
For several examples of the application of public history methods, see Dolores Hayden, *The Power of Place: Urban Landscapes as Public History*, (MIT Press, 1995).
Austin Allen, "Site of the Unseen: The Racial Gaming of the American Landscape," *Black Landscapes Matter*, ed. Walter Hood and Grace Mitchell Tada (University of Virginia Press, December 9, 2020), 100. Walter Hood, "Afterward," *Black Landscapes Matter*, ed.
Walter Hood and Grace Mitchell Tada (University of Virginia Press, December 9, 2020),

Gold Star Mining Co.
201-202 Wilson Block
Piute

Contradictions

Bringing the Past Forward©

barbara GOTHARD
November 22, 2021

The Homesteaders   Image Gallery   Time Lapses   Lanfair Valley Map   The Mojave Road   Detail: Lanfair tract

Created by

Jim Herries, Cartographer, ESRI and

Doug Morgenthaler, Program Manager, ESRI

https://storymaps.arcgis.com/stories/fc048a1491eb4895be37ceadfb9fb9a6

#1. Anna Jones 1872 –1915

Born: 1872 in Crawford County, Arkansas
6th of 10 children
Married: 1889 in Crawford County Arkansas
Husband: William Jones, born in Louisiana
as a slave, a farmer in Arkansas
Moved to Los Nietos, CA in 1907
Partner: Eldorado Gold Star Mining Company
Harts Township Corporation
Children: Ralph, Mabel, Golda, Mary Sidney,
Lonnie, Marie
Moved to Lanfair: 1910
Home: 12' x 14' on 163 acre tract
Died: 1915
Ralph, age 15 stayed on the homestead
3 children handed over to CA Probation
Office
Fellow homesteader, Howard Folke became
guardian for Lonnie and Marie

Crops: rye, corn, beans, milo maize, wheat

#2. John Richard Moulton 1853 – 1936

Born: 1853 in Missouri
Married: 1874 to Mollie Moulton for 26 years
No children
Owned Missouri house free and clear
1890: Moved to Los Angeles, CA
Described as 5'10" with dark eyes, dark hair
Worked as an Expressman, Laborer, Contractor and Teamster
Could read and write
1913: Incorporator for Dunbar Water Company
Built one room house in Lanfair
1915: Owned 160 acres plus 160 acres
1930: Moved to Los Angeles with brother, Warner Moulton

Crops: rye, corn, beans, wheat and oat hay, rye hay,
beans, milo maize, sudan grass

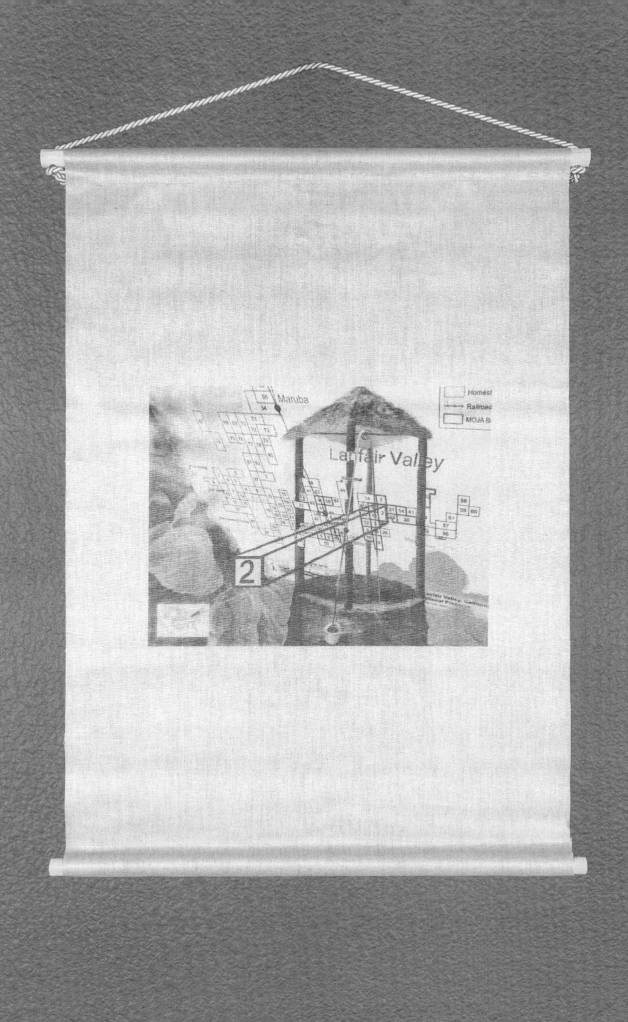

#3. John Massie 1848 – 1936

Born: 1848 in Frederick, Virginia
Married: Lou (born 1855) for 17 years
No children
Day Laborer
1900: Moved to Los Angeles, CA
1911: built Lanfair house
1912: Treasurer, Eldorado Gold Star Company
1914: Moved to Lanfair
1918: Filed lawsuit against Eldorado Gold
Star Mining Company regarding nonpayment of
promissory notes but apparently lost the case
One room house 8'x16'
Another building 15'x25' with 2 rooms
Chicken corral

Crops: barley, kaffir corn

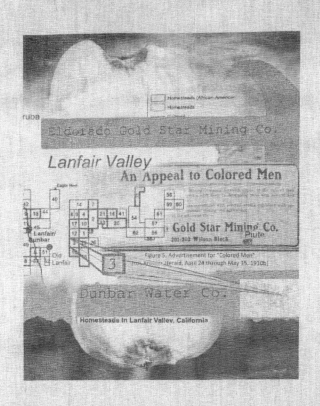

Homesteads (African American)
Homesteads

ruba

Eldorado Gold Star Mining Co.

Lanfair Valley

An Appeal to Colored Men

Gold Star Mining Co.
201-202 Wilson Block   Piute

Figure 5. Advertisement for "Colored Men"
[Los Angeles Herald, April 24 through May 15, 1910b]

Dunbar Water Co.

Homesteads in Lanfair Valley, California

#4. Lila Almonds Smith 1859 – 1950

Born: April 1859 into slavery in Texas
Married: Joseph Smith, 1881, Falls County, Texas
Seven children
1910: moved to Los Angeles
1911: Applied for Desert-Land Entry for $241.04
Improvements to land totaled $877
1913: Built house in Lanfair
House" 12'x12', floored and covered
Barn 10'x'10 with shed annexed
Had 1 workhorse
Hired Gershom Hodnett to seed and cultivate her
claim due to serious injury after being hit by a
motorcycle
Due to inability to obtain water from Western
Home and Water Association cultivating the land
was impossible.

Crops:potatoes, cabbage, onions

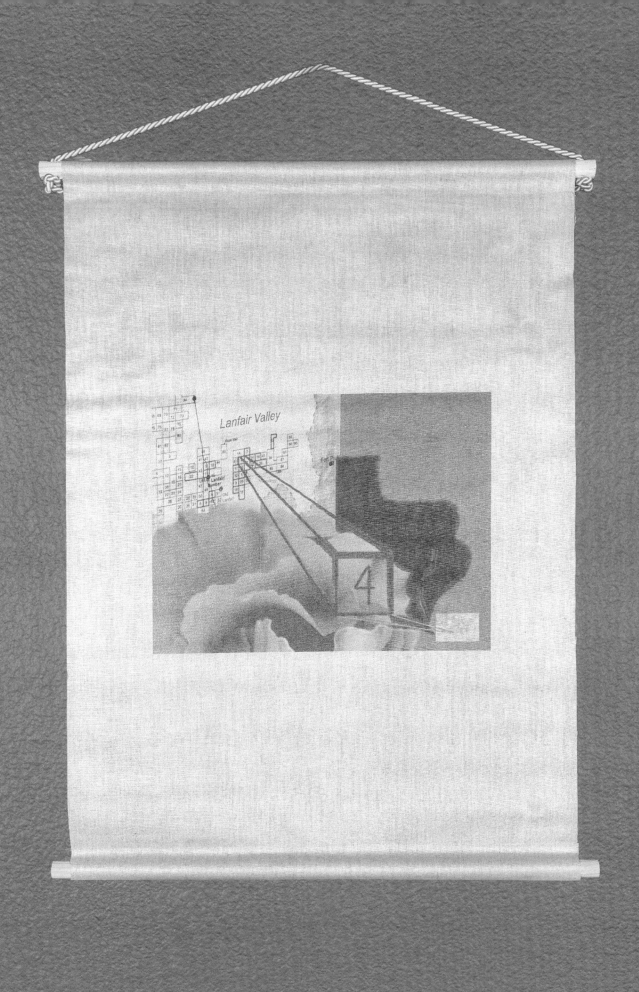

#5. Nathan Lowe 1887 - 1966

Born: September 5 in Georgia
One of 13 children
Occupation: Galvanizing
Tall, slender, brown eyes black hair
1912: filed for homestead
Married: Mary Shaw, Monrovia, CA
1914: Built house
1918: Lived in Los Angeles, CA
1920: Lived in Palo Verde, CA
1922: Received certificate for Patent
1930: Lived in Los Angeles, CA
Could read and write
1942: Lived in Los Angeles, CA

Crops: milo maize, barley

#6. Annie Taylor 1888 – unknown

Born: 1888 in Missouri
Married: Thomas Taylor, 1908 in Denver, CO
1912: Living in Pasedena, CA
Applied for homestead
Built 2-room house, shed, barn, corral
1913: Thomas died
1915: Filed for homestead
Application rejected due to early filing
submitted application, which was granted

Crops: maize corn, kaffir corn, potatoes, milo
maize, pumpkins, citrons, onions, fodder for horse

#7. Millard F. Bronson 1854 - 1920

Born: 1854 in Georgia into slavery, was literate
Married: Emma, 1875
Children: Lelia and Mattie
1888: Literate, could read and write
Registered voter
1889: Carpenter, Los Angeles County, CA
1894: Cabinet Maker, Alameda, CA
Married: Mary Kate Williams
1911: Applied for homestead $275
Tenant farmer
1912-1916: Built house and lived in Lanfair, CA
2 rooms, board and batten tar paper roof (value $150)
Barn: Made of lumber, 14'x14' (value $25)
Chicken house and toilet (value $10)
1916: Moved to Los Angeles, CA
Worked as a carpenter
1917: Sold his homestead to Mattie and Taylor Morgan

Crops: corn rye, milo maize, kaffir corn, watermelons, wheat

#8. Robert E. Edwards 1865 - 1935

Born: 1865 in Georgia
Married: 1895, Georgia V
Children: Anna, born in Ohio 1906
Samuel, born in A 1907
1913: Applied for homestead
1914: Lived in Monrovia, CA, moved to Lanfair
1918: Final proof
1920: Monrovia, Los Angles, CA
Owned home with mortgage (Value $5000)
Can read and write
1922: Lived in Lanfair, granted patent
1923: Laborer, rancher, gardener
1935: Nov 15, Los Angeles

Crops: milo maize, oats

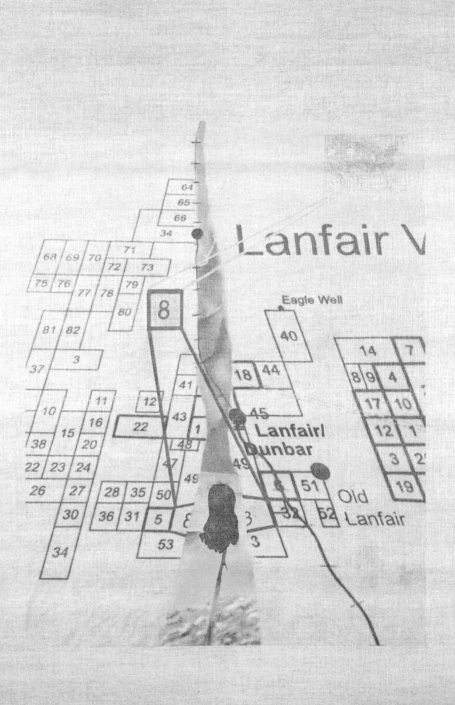

#9. William C Williams 1867 – 1940

Born: 1867 in Texas
Married: 1900 Ada
1910: Could read and write
3rd grade education
Children: gave birth to 1 child, 0 survived
Laborer, car shop
1913: Built house
1915: Applied for homestead
Established residency, September 26
1916: Registered voter in Lanfair, Republican
Rancher
1918: Lived in Lanfair
1920: Lived in Venice, Madison, Illinois
Owned house, valued at $200

Ada Owned house, valued at $100

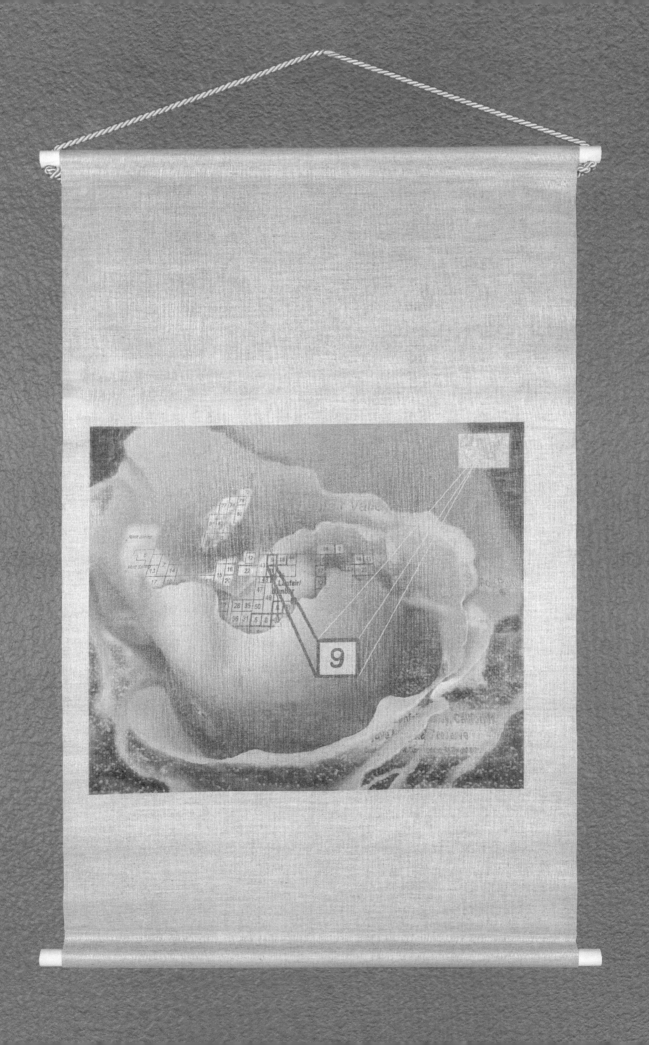

#10. Richard Wesley Hodnett, Sr. 1851 – 1940

Born: 1851 in Troup County Georgia
Born into slavery
Married: four times
1. 1870-1870 Emma Day
Children: William Warren
Fannie
2. 1880 Amanda
Children: William, Fannie, John and Estella
3. 1890 Luella Perry
Children: Bessie (1891-1975)
Matthew (1893-1915)
Zipporah (1894-1972)
Stephen (1896-1993)
Gershom (1898-1968)
Rosetta (1901-1975)
Sarah (1902 -2000)
Luella (1902 est.-1906)
4. 1906 Susie Willis, worked at Goff's hotel
Children: Jennie (1907-1940)
Richard Wesley, Jr. (1908-2003)
Florence (1910-1918)
Farmer and worked as cook on train
Religion: Seventh Day Adventist
1910: Los Nietos, CA
Applied for homestead
1913: Built 4-room house, stable and chicken house.
1917: Moved to Needles then to Blyth
1940: November 24, Los Angeles County

Crops: corn, rye, cane, vegetables

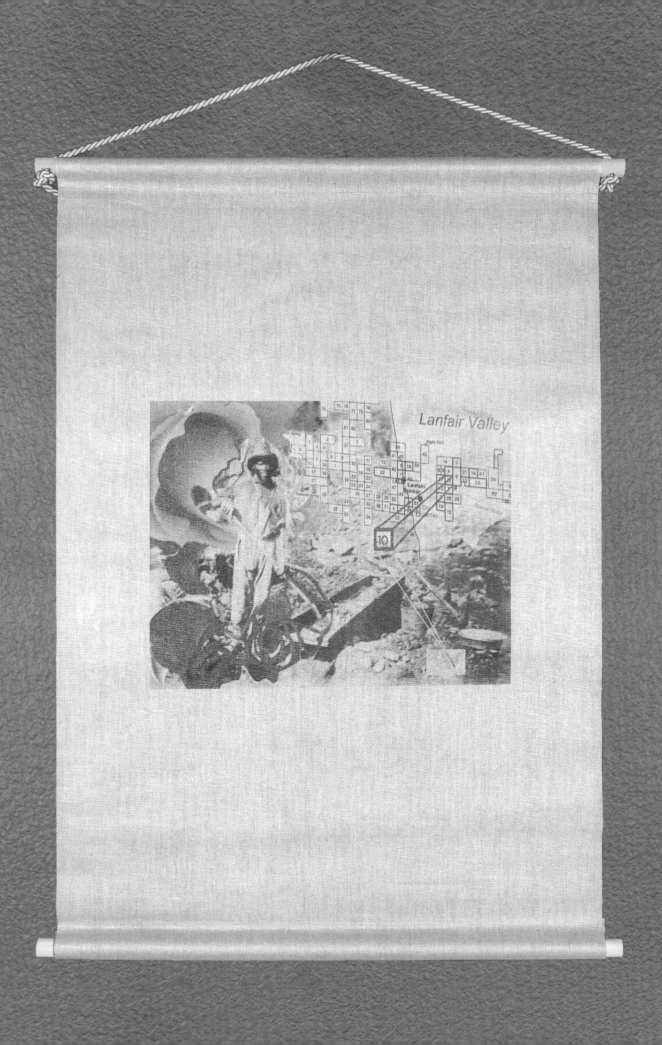

#11. Stonewall Jackson 1865 – 1950

Born: 1865 in Georgia
1910: Lived in Los Angeles
Widowed
Worked as a chauffeur
Literate
1913: Applied for his homestead and established
residence
2-room house (12x18 ft, floored and covered
barn (9x16 ft, covered)
1914: Married Ethel Jackson
1915: House burned down
Religious activity: Jacksons attended church and
Sunday school with the Craigs

Crops: wheat, kaffir corn, wheat hay, corn, corn
fodder
cane

#12. Ulysses Simpson Hodnett 1884 - 1961

Born: 1884 in Crawford County Arkansas
Father: Alexander Hodnett and Laura Appleby
Nephew: Richard Wesley Hodnett, Sr.
1908: Moved to CA
Applied for homestead at age 29
1914: Built a 1-room house
1919: Married Mary Brown in Los Angeles County
1930: Moved to Phoenix, Arizona
1940: Moved to Stockton, CA
1961: Died in San Joaquin County, CA

Crops: corn, pumpkins, rye, corn, cane

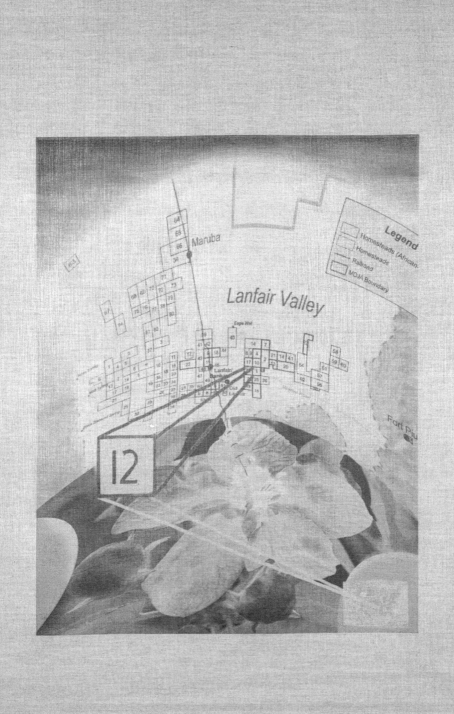

#13. John David Jones 1868 – 1920

Born: 1868 in Kentucky
1865: Married Myrtle Cushingberry in Douglas County, Kansas
One child who may have died
1895: Lived in Lawrence, Douglas County Kansas
1900: Lived in Topeka, Kansas
1905: Lived in Rutland, Montgomery County, Kansas
1910: Lived in Pasedena, CA
1913: Applied for Homestead and lived in Dunbar, California
Built 4-room house (20x20 ft, floored and covered)
Chicken house (9x9 ft, covered)
One well (114 ft deep and 4x4 1/2ft);
Another well (30 ft deed and 4 1/2 ft, two cisterns, each
60 barrel capacity, $1100)
Established residence
1920: Moved to Los Angeles, CA

Crops: sudan grass, timothy grass, rape, oats,
Indian corn, beans, kaffir corn sudan grace

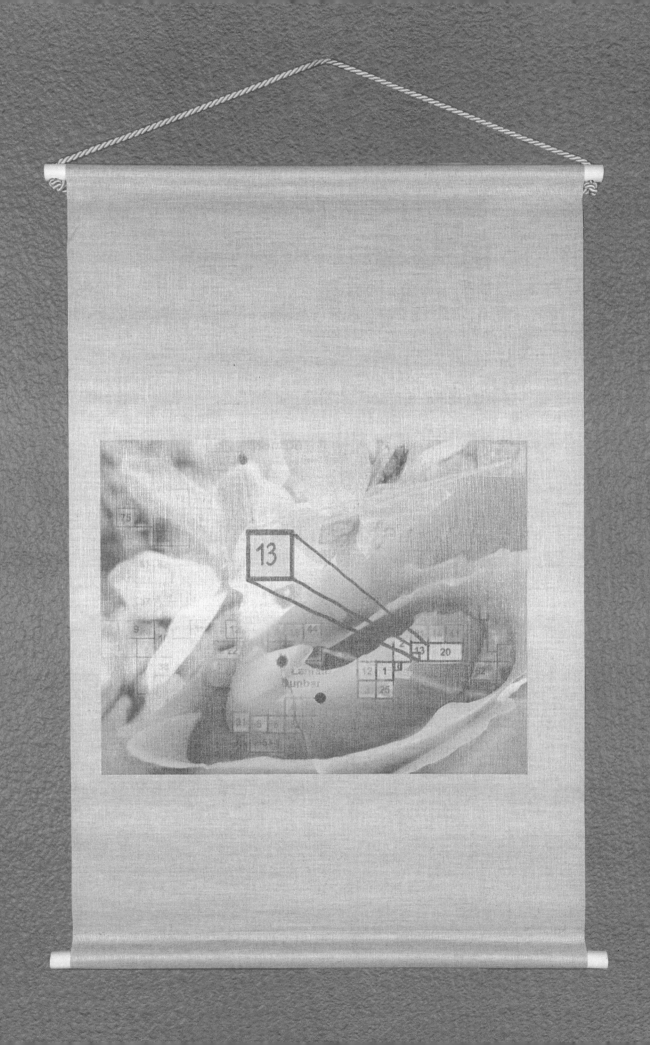

#14. Millie C. Sheppard-Grady 1880 - 1918

Born: 1880 in Wedowee, Alabama
Family affiliation with other homesteaders:
Third cousin of Richard Wesley Hodnett, Sr. and
Lavinia Massie, wife of John Massie
Religious affiliation: Seventh Day Adventist
1900: Lived in Wedowee, Alabama with parents,
John and Ellen Sheppard
1910: Lived in Stillwater, Minnesota with her parents
1913: Lived in Los Angeles with her parents
Filed for homestead
Built home, 2-room house (12x16 ft, the other
room 6x9 ft., covered), chicken house (5x6 ft.
covered)
1914: Established residence
Filed additional homestead application
1915: Married in San Bernardino County, CA to
Wiley Grady (born in Kentucky) and moved to Lanfair
1916: Living in Lanfair
1917: Granted patent
1918: Los Angeles, CA

Crops: rye, corn, beans, milo maize, wheat, corn

#15. Hattie Morton 1850 - 1950

Born: 1850 in Missouri
Female, black, keeping house
1870: Married Henry Morton 22, black, farm
hand,
could not read or write
Mary M, daughter, attended school in
Missouri
Cammie, Mother-in-law, widowed
1900: Lived in Los Angeles, CA
Owned house free and clear
Hay feeder
1910: Rented house in Los Angeles
1914: Established residence in Lanfair
One-room house (12x13) floored and covered,
barn (15x20 ft.), covered
1917: Final Homestead proof submitted
1920: Widowed, lived in Los Angeles
1921: Received certificate for Patent

Crops: milo maize, wheat

#16. Estella Hodnett Baker 1881 - 1918

Born: 1881 in Arkansas
Father: Richard Wesley Hodnett, Sr. and his
Mother: second wife Amanda Appleby (died est. 1884)
1900: Lived in Van Buren, Arkansas with father and
stepmother Luella Perry
1905: Married George Baker, Kansas
Children: Herschel, Harold, and Mildred
1910-1913: George and Mildred died
1913: Applied for homestead
1914: Established residency
Built one-room house
1914-1917: Richard Wesley Hodnett, Sr. and Ulysses
Hodnett checked on sons when Estella was away
from the land.
1918: Richard Wesley Hodnett, Sr. assumed
guardianship of sons
1922: Patent granted posthumously probably to
Richard Wesley Hodnett, Sr., on behalf of two sons

Crops: corn, pumpkins, rye, corn, cane

#17. William Warren Hodnett 1859 - 1956

Born: 1859 in Georgia
Eldest son of Richard Wesley Hodnett, Sr.
First wife, Emma Day
Lived in Georgia
Lived in Alabama with father and step-mother,
        Amanda Appleby
Grandfather, Warren Hodnett
1880: Lived in Hampton, Lee County, Arkansas
1897: Moved to Van Buren, Crawford County, Arkansas
Four children: Jemina, Jethro, Emma, and Zurula
Owned farm free and clear near grandfather Warren
Hodnett
1909: Daughter, Margaret, born in CA
1913: Lived in Watts, CA
Applied for homestead
Established residency
1914: Built two-room house
1920: Lived in Los Angeles, CA with his wife and 14
            children
1956: January 26 in Ontario, CA

Crops: corn, wheat, rye, wheat hay, cane

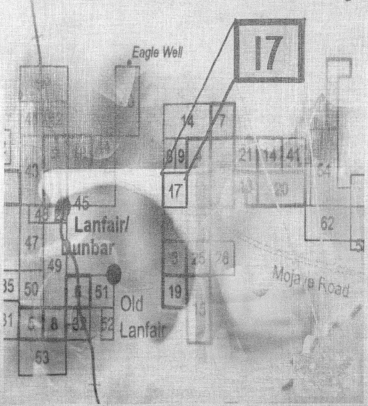

Lanfair Valley

Eagle Well

17

14 7

8 9

21 14 41 54

17

80

62

45

Lanfair/
Dunbar

47

49

Mojave Road

35 50 5 61

Old
Lanfair

19

53

#18. Matthew Hodnett 1893 – 1915

Born: 1893 in Crawford County, Arkansas
Father: Richard Wesley Hodnett, Sr.
Mother: Luella Perry (third wife)
1900: Lived in Van Buren, Crawford County,
Arkansas
Nine siblings
1910: Moved to Los Nietos, CA
Stepmother: Suzie Willis
Nine siblings
1914: Filed for Homestead in Lan fair Valley
Built one-room house
1915: Died, Needles, CA
1917: Richard Wesley Hodnett, Sr., submitted
final proof on Mathew's behalf as his heir
1922: Patent granted to his heirs

Crops: corn, cane, rye

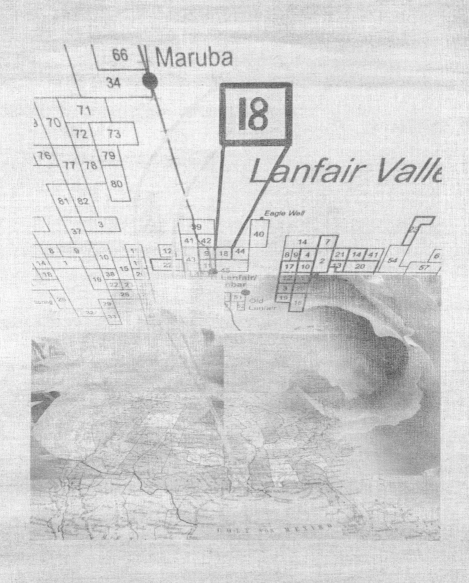

#19. William H. Carter 1844 - 1926

Born: 1844 in Fairfax County, Virginia
Black, farm laborer, could not read or write
1864: Enlisted in Company D, US Army 23rd Regiment
Colored Infantry Volunteers*
1870: Married Lydia
Black, keeping house, could not read or write
Children: Ellen (could not read nor write),
James, William
1915: Applied for Homestead
Lived in Alhambra, widower with 3 children
1916: Submitted final proof
Lived in Lanfair
1917: Received certificate for Patent
1920: Lived in Alhambra, Los Angeles, CA
Rented house
Widowed
Could not read or write
Housecleaner for private family
1926: March 27, Was in Soldiers Home in Sawtelle, CA
prior to his prior to his death

Crops: wheat, oats, vegetables
*A Civil War Veteran

#20. Nanie Mary Craig 1873 - 1935

Born: 1873 in Ghent, Carroll, Kentucky
Mulatto
Farmer
Attended school, Literate
Niece: Roberta B., OH
Nephew: Robert N., OH
1915: Applied for homestead
Lived in Pasedena, CA
Housekeeper
1916: Brother: Jessie Craig and wife Willa lived in
Lanfair for 5 months
Homestead: George Lindsay worked for Nannie on her
homestead
1918: Submitted final proof
1921: Granted patent
1922: Registered to Vote in Pasedena, CA (Republican)
Working as a maid
Still owned property in Lanfair
1930: Lived in San Bernardino, CA
Owned house valued at $2,000
Could read and write
1934: Registered to vote in San Bernardino, CA
(Republican)
Rancher
!935:Died
1984: 20 acres sold to Ray Furness (date unknown)
1984: Remaining 300 acres, divided into 60-acre
parcels for six relatives
1985: Robert W. Craig started building a house
Moved mobile home onto parcel while building a two-
story house of rock or stone
House destroyed by wind
Well put on property

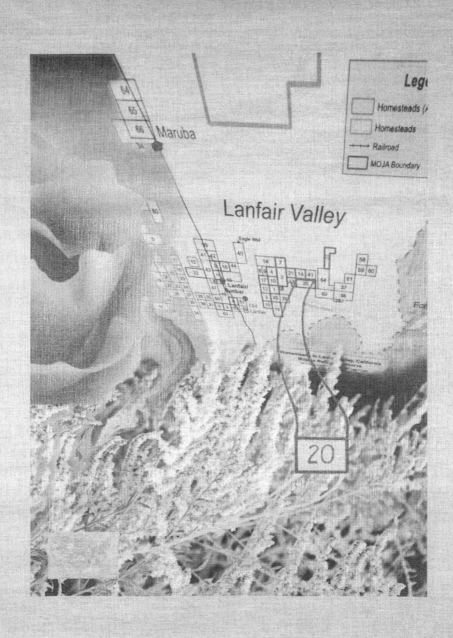

#21. Alfred Summers 1848 - 1925

Born: 1848 in Virginia
1873: Enlisted as Private in F Company, 10th Calvary
in Washington, D.C.
Served as one of the Buffalo Soldiers
Gray horses
1978: Discharged from military at Fort Concho, TX
End of service, November 12
1880: Married, Millie Summers
No children
Married 30 years
1895: Granted Patent, Mount Diablo Meridian, CA,
located in Amador County, CA
1896: Lived in Pasadena, CA
5'10". colored, black eyes, black hair
Laborer
Odd jobs
Owned house free and clear
Could read and write
1915: Applied for Soldiers Homestead Entry in Lanfair Valley
1916: Millie died, Los Angeles County, CA
1917: Filed final proof
1920: Lived in Lanfair, CA
1922: Provided discharge papers to land office
Granted Patent
1923: Lived in Pasadena, CA
1925: Admitted to US National Home for Disabled
Volunteer Soldiers, Pacific Branch, Sawtelle, CA

Crops: barley, cane

#22. George Lindsay 1860 - 1935

Born: 1860 in Missouri
1881: Married to Julia
1916: Established residence in house built by
former entryman
1917: Applied for homestead (rejected)
1920: Owned farm
Black
Could read and write
8th grade education
Dairyman, Farmer
1923: Lived in Los Angeles, CA
Applied for homestead
1924: Submitted final proof (rejected)
1925: Certificate of Patent issued
Four-room house (18x26 ft. floored and covered
with porch), shed (10x10), barn (18x36 ft.) covered
Cost of improvements $800
1930: Lived in San Antonio
Owned house valued at $2000
Widowed
Laborer, General building construction
1935: Lived in San Antonio, Los Angeles, CA
1935: Died

Crops: oats, sudan grass, corn, melons, truck garden

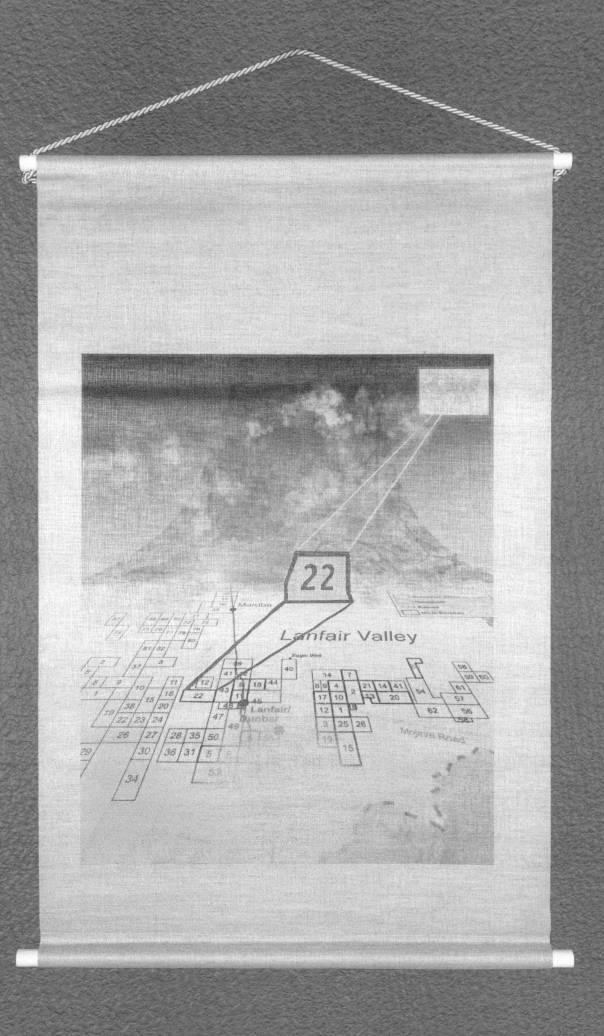

#23. Howard Frank Carter 1881 - 1935

Born: 1881 in Fairfax County, Virginia
Barber
Native born, colored, medium build, brown eyes,
black hair
Brother, William H. Carter, Alhambra, CA
1899: Married, May Bell Ohmstead in Harrison County, OH
Black
1 child who did not survive
Housewife
1918: Registered for WWI Draft
Lived in Oxnard, Ventura, CA
Tractor engineer for P.A, Rice
1920: Lived in Oxnard, Ventura, CA
Rented home
Registered to vote (Republican)
1924: Applied for homestead
Established residence and built house
20x40 ft. included 800 ties ($800), two story
chicken house 8x19 ($250), barn, corral and garage ($300)
Lived an registered to vote in Lanfair, CA
1925-1926: Lived in Lanfair, CA
1928: House burned to ground Nov 15 while they were away
1929: Submitted final proof
Lived in Needles, CA
1930: Granted Patent
1934: Lived and registered to vote in Needles, CA
Democrat
Janitor

Crops: barley, wheat, milo maize

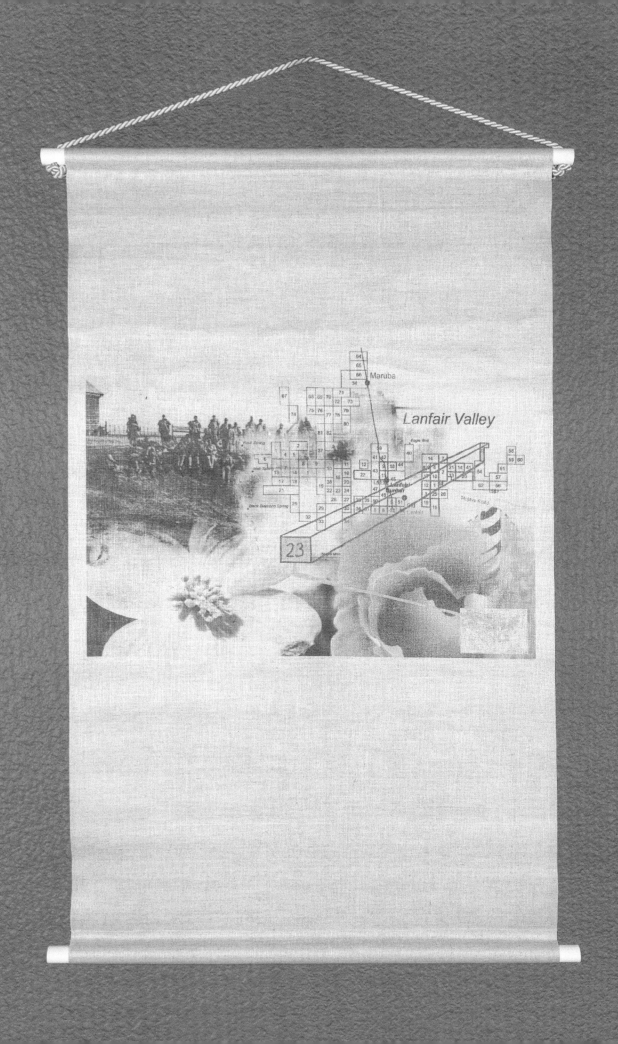

Row 1, Lanfair/Dunbar archaeological objects courtesy of Mojave National Preserve; Row 2, Development of the prototype for the linen panels in artist's studio; Linen panels before installation; Craig Putnam, Exhibit Fabricator, map replication installation; Row 3, Public Programs, San Bernardino County Museum, 2022

About the Artist

Photo Credit: Nettie Peña

As a woman artist of color living in the Mojave Desert area, Gothard is part of a small population of African American residents and artists who recently settled here. So when she first discovered information about the twenty three African American families who settled in the Mojave Desert in 1910 she was determined to share their stories. She felt compelled to visually communicate the continuity she felt with the contradiction of the original African American homesteaders in the desert and to expand her outreach by engaging with and educating today's communities about these homesteader's history.

Gothard's focus for this installation and catalogue is to pay homage to the African American homesteaders who once farmed the Mojave Desert in the context of her own uniqueness as a recent settler in the Mojave's expanding productive land. She unlocked an unconscious kinship that inspires her to develop visual interpretations of her own life, consistent with her contemporary artworks that explore subliminal messages revealing the unconscious mind — dreams, motivations and memories — and sometimes autobiographical.

Gothard's challenge in developing *Contradictions -Bringing The Past Forward* was to develop her innovative concept of creating on her iPad an Art + Humanities project consisting of twenty three digital paintings, tract map replica, story map and site specific archeological objects while imparting the historical, cultural and personal significance of these homesteaders of color that were invited to the more inhospitable regions of the San Bernardino County so long ago. She utilized her traditional art training at Mount Mary University (Bachelors), Long Island University (Masters) and Michigan State University (Ph.D) and her historical influencers (Bosch, Vermeer, Klimt, O'Keeffe, and Gerzo) while staying true to her own style of using striking color combinations that appear restful and yet come across with power, images that are complex and mystical found in her large oil scale oil paintings.

Contradictions - Bringing The Past Forward is the most current evolution of her art practice which results from a lifetime of life-altering experiences that inform all of her artworks: an investigation of contradictions as the foundation her unique lived experiences - a career path that zigzagged from artist/art teacher/administrator to international corporate executive to artist.

She is an artist, art magazine writer/contributor whose artworks are exhibited regionally, nationally and internationally and are in private and institutional collections. Gothard's commitment to community service is an integral part of her life. She is currently a member of the Board of Trustees, Palm Springs Art Museum and an Emeritus Member of the Artists Council, having previously served on non-profit, business association and corporate boards.

BLOG:
MojaveContradictions.com

Contradictions - Bringing The Past Forward
evolved during COVID restrictions in 2020 as
I reflected on the contradictions of being an
African American female artist who lives in
the Mojave Desert area. My Blog,
MojaveContradictions.com provides narratives
about the project beginning with my accidental
research discoveries.

My discoveries of these homesteaders
reminded me of a book that has always
intrigued me, *The Three Princes of Serendip* -
the English version of the story Peregrinaggio
di tre giovani figliuoli del re di Serendippoby,
Venice in 1757. The story emanated from
Cristoforo Armeno, who had translated the
original 1302 Persian fairy tale into Italian.
According to the blog, *Are Arte et Labor* (*Art
Skill and Work*), in the English speaking world
this story is known as a source of the word
serendipity which Horace Walpole is thought
to have originated. The three princes by
"accidents and sagacity" were to discern the
nature of a lost camel.

July 24, 2022

**The Mojave Project
DISPATCH now live**

November 10, 2021

**Artist Talk –
BoxoPROJECTS Artist
Residency**

February 5, 2022

**Untethered: Desert
Residencies Panel
Discussion**

October 13, 2021

**Copper Mountain College
Hosts Visual
Interpretation**

October 12, 2021

**Desert Institute Second
Friday Lecture Series**

June 7, 2022

**"Contradictions" at
Victor Valley Museum**

April 23, 2022

**Mil-Tree's Spoken Word
Event: Live From Joshua
Tree**

July 19, 2022

**Join us for THE MOJAVE
PROJECT 2022 WEBINAR
SERIES**

Public Programming

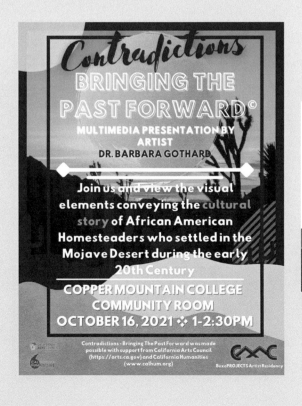

For Further Reading

African American Artists 1910

https://en.wikipedia.org/wiki/List_of_African-American_visual_artists

African American Civil Rights Network, National Park Service

https://www.nps.gov/subjects/civilrights/african-american-civil-rights-network.htm

African American History Timeline, Black Past

https://www.blackpast.org/african-american-history-timeline/

African American Homesteading in the Mojave Desert Report, 1910 -1930, Collaboration National Park Service, Fort Lewis College, and Applied Cultural Ecology, LLC, National Park Service Cultural Anthropology Program

https://www.nps.gov/places/california-mojave-national-preserve-lanfair-settlement-archive.htm

Ancestry.com

https://www.blackpast.org/african-american-history-timeline/

Ann Japenga, California Desert Art

https://www.californiadesertart.com/

Black Homesteader Project, University of Nevada Las Vegas

https://www.unl.edu/plains/black-homesteader-project

California Homesteader Project, Guinda

https://california.hometownlocator.com/

Chris Clarke, African-Americans Shaping the California Desert: Homesteading in the Mojave KECT.org

Chris Clarke, Coyote Crossing, JCET TV LA

D. Scot Miller, Call it Afro-Surreal

https://sfbgarchive.48hills.org/sfbgarchive/2009/05/19/call-it-afro-surreal/,Volume 43 Number 34, May 19, 2009

Deborah Willis, The Black Civil War Soldier: A visual History of Conflict & Citizenship, NYU Press, Series in Social and Cultural Analysis, January 26, 2021

https://nyupress.org/9781479809004/the-black-civil-war-soldier/

Dennis G. Casebier and Mojave Road Guide: Tales of the Mojave Road, Number 11, June 1986, pp 72 - 86

https://mdhca.org/

Environmental Service Research Institute, (ESRI),

https://www.esri.com/

George Washington Carver National Monument

https://www.nps.gov/gwca/index.htm

George Washington Carver

https://en.wikipedia.org/wiki/George_Washington_Carver

For Further Reading (continued)

Joe Blackstock, The untold story: African American homesteaders once farmed the Mojave Desert, Daily Bulletin

dailybulletin.com

Jacob Lawrence, The Great Migration Series, Museum of Modern Art

moma.org

Map, Jesse W. Tune, 2-5-21

https://www.nps.gov/moja/index.htm

Mexican Muralism, The Art Story

https://www.theartstory.org/movement/mexican-muralism/history-and-concepts

Mojave Desert Heritage & Cultural Association,

mdhca.org

Mojave Reader, Volume 1 Dispatch, "Experiments In Desert Utopic Living, Kim Stringfellow, 2021, p.56-65

https://mojaveproject.org/dispatches-item/experiments-desert-utopic-living/

Oscar Micheaux

https://en.wikipedia.org/wiki/Oscar_Micheaux

Newspapers.com

https://www.newspapers.com/

Nikki

https://thebolditalic.com/the-long-erased-history-of-californias-black-settlersc28903056ce2

Steve Lech, The Branding Iron, Los Angeles Corral of the Westerners, Winter 2015, Number 277

https://www.worldcat.org/title/branding-iron/oclc/2788777

The Conquest,

https://books.google.com/books/about/The_Conquest.html?id=A9CJ_dPnd18C

The Homesteader, Netflix

https://www.cnet.com/news/black-history-month-2021-how-oscarmicheaux-defied-hollywood-tomake-the-homesteader/

The Long-Erased History of California's Earliest Black Residents; Feb 1, 2021

https://thebolditalic.com/the-long-erased-history-of-californias-black-settlers-c28903056ce2

The Mojave Road is California's off-roading mecca, Matt Jaffe, San Francisco Chronicle, March 23, 2018

https://www.sfchronicle.com/travel/article/The-Mojave-Road-is-California-s-off-roading-12776695.php

Untold Stories: Black Lives Unmasked, Orange County Bar Association

https://oclba.org/2020/07/28/ocba-town-hall-untold-stories/

U.S. National Archives

https://www.archives.gov

Acknowledgements

None of us live in a vacuum and no person is an island.* *Contradictions - Bringing The Past Forward* would not have been possible without the guidance, support, and encouragement of many people.

Essay Contributors

Phoebe Beasley, Artist
Melissa Russo, Executive Director (ret.), San Bernardino County Museum

Installation Support

Rebecca Austin and Ginny Bengston, Department of Anthropology, Fort Lewis College, Study Authors
Stephen Richard Baumbach, Printer/Photographer
Aimee Buyea, Art Consultant
Dennis Casebier,** "Pioneer" researcher considered to be an initial source of information
Robert Crouch, Executive Director, Fulcrum Arts
Ann Marie Gothard, Editorial Support
Diana Rodriguez, Event Support
Donald Gothard, Jr., Tech Support
Barbara Gothard, Creative Concept
Jim Herries, Cartography, ArcGIS Living Atlas, ESRI
Ellen Knable, Volunteer
Bernard Leibov, Director, BoxoPROJECTS Artist Residency
Doug Morgenthaler, Senior Product Engineering Lead, ESRI
Nettie Peña, Photographer
David R. Nichols, Park Archeologist, Cultural Resources Program Manager, Mojave National Preserve, Castle Mountains National Monument, National Park service, Commissioned the *African American Homesteading in the Mojave Desert 1910 - 1930 Study*
Rod Sexton, Photographer
Joe Toenjes, Archeologist, Mojave National Preserve
Leigh Wiemann, Editorial Consultant
The amazing San Bernardino County Museum Staff
    Melissa Russo, Executive Director, (ret.)
    David Myers, Executive Director
    Jennifer McCormick, Marketing Specialist
    Craig Putnam, Exhibit Fabricator
    Ashley Lothyan, Curator of Art & Museum Education
    Jennifer Dickerson, Museum Curator, History
    Tiffany Talavera, Associate Curator Victor Valley Museum
    Eliana Zacharias, Education Coordinator
    Zachary Tucker, Executive Director, San Bernardino County Museum Association

*Thomas Merton
**Deceased

Special thanks to
Raul Ruiz, M.D., Member of the U.S. House of Representatives,
California Congressional District 36, 117th Congress
for Certificate of Congressional Recognition

Contradictions - Bringing The Past Forward© made possible with support from California Humanities, a non-profit partner of National Endowment for the Humanities

CALIFORNIA HUMANITIES

www.calhum.org Learn More

Contradictions - Bringing The Past Forward© is funded in part by the California Arts Council, a state agency

CALIFORNIA ARTS COUNCIL A STATE AGENCY

https://arts.ca.gov Learn More

Index

Published about the 2022 exhibition

Contradictions - Bringing The Past Forward

Presented at
San Bernardino County Museum in Redlands, California
Apple Valley Museum, Victor Valley, California

Cover front: *#3 John Massie 1848 -1936* (2021), detail
Cover back: *#6 Annie Taylor 1888 - unknown* (2021), detail
Frontispiece: Exhibition Title Panel: *Contradictions -Bringing The Past Forward*
San Bernardino County Museum, Redlands, California

ISBN: 978-1-916770-51-5

Publisher Gothard Fine Art

Editor: Barbara Gothard

Printing
United States of America

Printed in the USA
CPSIA information can be obtained
at www.ICGtesting.com
LVRC080726090923
757724LV00019B/73